CONTENTS

Japan Unlocked: A Short Guide to Travelling and Selling in Japan	1
Chapter 1: The Geography and Culture of Japan	5
Chapter 2: The Logistics of Travelling in Japan	11
Chapter 3: Setting Up Your Business in Japan	17
Chapter 4: What to Sell in Japan: Market Insights	24
Chapter 5: Selling Industrial Products and Services in Japan	30
Chapter 6: Selling at Markets and Fairs in Japan	37
Chapter 7: Selling Online in Japan	44
Chapter 8: Marketing Strategies for Japanese Consumers	51
Chapter 9: Navigating Japanese Business Etiquette	58
Chapter 10: Conclusion – Unlocking Success in Japan	64
About The Author	71

JAPAN UNLOCKED: A SHORT GUIDE TO TRAVELLING AND SELLING IN JAPAN

J K Lewis

Introduction

Japan is a captivating blend of ancient traditions and cutting-edge innovation, where centuries-old temples stand alongside modern skyscrapers, and quiet tea houses coexist with bustling urban centres. Known for its high standards of quality, meticulous attention to detail, and discerning consumers, Japan has earned a reputation as one of the most sophisticated and unique markets in the world. For businesses willing to adapt to local preferences and uphold these values, Japan presents significant opportunities for success.

With its highly developed infrastructure, advanced e-commerce sector, and a society that values both tradition and technological progress, Japan offers a dynamic environment for entrepreneurs. This guide will explore the essential aspects of entering and succeeding in the Japanese market, from understanding consumer culture to navigating logistics, adhering to local regulations, and building lasting relationships with Japanese partners.

Why Japan?

Japan is the world's third-largest economy and a global leader in innovation, known for industries ranging from automotive and electronics to fashion and beauty. The Japanese consumer market is unique in its high standards, as customers are deeply quality-conscious, brand-loyal, and value detail and authenticity. This discerning approach extends to all aspects of life, from the way goods are packaged to the service experiences provided. For businesses prepared to meet these expectations, Japan offers a high-potential market for long-term growth.

The rise of e-commerce and digital engagement has created additional opportunities, particularly for brands looking to tap into the tech-savvy younger population and Japan's burgeoning online shopping habits. Moreover, Japan's influence on global pop culture, particularly through anime, gaming, and fashion, offers brands the chance to build international appeal by establishing a presence in this influential market.

What You'll Learn

In this guide, we'll cover each key aspect of travelling, selling, and building a successful business in Japan, providing you with the strategies, insights, and tools to thrive in this dynamic and competitive market. We'll cover:

- **Understanding Japanese consumer culture**: Explore how Japan's focus on quality, attention to detail, and value of tradition influence consumer behaviour across the country's diverse regions.

- **Travelling and logistics**: From Japan's efficient transport network to accommodation and inventory management, discover the most convenient ways to travel and handle logistics for your business in Japan.

- **Setting up your business**: From choosing the right business structure to understanding tax obligations and compliance, we'll guide you through each step of establishing a legal and reputable business presence in Japan.

- **Selling at markets and fairs**: Japan has a rich culture of markets and fairs that offer direct access to consumers. Learn how to apply for stalls, set up an attractive display, and engage with customers in Japan's famous markets.

- **Building a strong online presence**: With a tech-savvy population and a thriving e-commerce market, Japan presents a strong digital opportunity. Discover how to create an online presence optimised for Japanese consumers, from website localisation to choosing the right e-commerce platforms.

- **Effective marketing strategies**: Delve into the marketing channels that work best in Japan, from social media and influencer marketing to SEO and traditional advertising. Tailor your brand messaging to resonate with Japanese audiences and reach a loyal customer base.

- **Navigating Japanese business etiquette**: In Japan, business is as much about trust and respect as it is about products and services. Understand the importance of formality, communication styles, and building relationships in Japanese business culture to establish credibility and trust.

Opportunities and Challenges

Japan's market offers immense opportunities but also demands a commitment to quality, service, and adaptability. Japanese consumers are known for being brand-loyal but selective, favouring businesses that go the extra mile to deliver exceptional products and experiences. Adapting your approach to align with Japanese values and consistently meeting these high expectations will be crucial for achieving success.

Embrace the Journey

Succeeding in Japan requires more than just bringing great products to market—it demands an understanding of Japanese culture, an ability to build relationships, and a dedication to quality. By following this guide, you'll gain the insights, strategies, and tools to unlock the full potential of the Japanese market. Whether you're establishing your brand online, setting up a stall at a local market, or forming partnerships with Japanese companies, this guide is designed to equip you for a successful journey in Japan.

CHAPTER 1: THE GEOGRAPHY AND CULTURE OF JAPAN

Japan's culture is a unique blend of ancient customs and cutting-edge modernity. From the bustling cityscapes of Tokyo and Osaka to the tranquil countryside and traditional villages, each region has its own distinct character and consumer preferences. Understanding Japan's regional diversity, cultural values, and the influences that shape consumer behaviour will provide a strong foundation for successfully navigating this complex and sophisticated market.

In this chapter, we'll explore Japan's primary regions, the differences between urban and rural consumer markets, and the core cultural values that guide Japanese consumer decisions.

1.1 Overview of Japan's Regions

Japan consists of four main islands—Honshu, Hokkaido, Kyushu, and Shikoku—each with its own unique culture, climate, and economic strengths. The key regions of Japan each have distinct characteristics, which can impact consumer preferences and business practices.

Tokyo – The Capital and Economic Powerhouse

- **Overview**: As the capital city, Tokyo is Japan's largest and most dynamic metropolitan area. It's a global business hub, renowned for its technology, finance, fashion, and cultural influence. Tokyo residents tend to be trend-conscious, tech-savvy, and highly receptive to international brands.
- **Key Industries**: Tokyo is a centre for technology, finance, fashion, and entertainment. The city is also

at the forefront of innovation, with consumers often seeking high-quality, cutting-edge products.

- **Consumer Preferences**: Tokyo consumers are willing to invest in premium products and are quick to adopt new trends. They appreciate products that emphasise quality, innovation, and design, especially those that offer convenience or reflect current trends in fashion or technology.

Osaka – The Friendly and Pragmatic City

- **Overview**: Located in the Kansai region, Osaka is Japan's second-largest city and is known for its hospitality and pragmatic approach to business. The city has a strong culture of entrepreneurship and is a commercial hub with a focus on food, manufacturing, and retail.
- **Key Industries**: Osaka is renowned for its food industry, textiles, electronics, and retail. The city is a major player in the Japanese manufacturing sector and is known for its vibrant business community.
- **Consumer Preferences**: Osaka consumers tend to be price-conscious yet value quality. They are loyal to brands they trust but are also open to trying new products, particularly if they offer a good balance of quality and cost-efficiency.

Kyoto – Japan's Cultural Heartland

- **Overview**: Known as Japan's cultural centre, Kyoto is famous for its temples, shrines, and traditional arts. This city attracts both locals and international tourists who are interested in experiencing Japan's traditional culture.
- **Key Industries**: Tourism, traditional crafts, hospitality, and local food products. Kyoto is a significant centre for artisanal goods and traditional Japanese crafts, such as ceramics, textiles, and tea.

- **Consumer Preferences**: Kyoto consumers appreciate artisanal goods, cultural authenticity, and sustainable practices. Products that showcase Japanese heritage, quality craftsmanship, or a connection to nature are particularly well-received.

Fukuoka – Emerging Tech and Start-Up Hub

- **Overview**: Located in Kyushu, Fukuoka has become known as a growing centre for start-ups and technology companies. It has a younger demographic and a thriving business environment that encourages innovation.
- **Key Industries**: Tech, start-ups, retail, and food. Fukuoka has seen significant investment in technology, making it a popular destination for businesses in IT, e-commerce, and innovation-driven sectors.
- **Consumer Preferences**: Fukuoka consumers are open to new ideas and products, with a strong interest in technology and digital experiences. Younger consumers in particular are trend-conscious and appreciate brands that offer a unique or innovative approach.

1.2 Urban vs. Rural Markets

Urban and rural markets in Japan exhibit distinct differences in consumer behaviour and product preferences. While urban consumers are more receptive to international brands and new trends, rural consumers tend to favour local brands, traditional products, and sustainable practices.

Urban Markets

- **Key Characteristics**: Japan's urban areas, particularly Tokyo, Osaka, and Fukuoka, are fast-paced, trend-sensitive, and brand-conscious. Consumers in these cities are accustomed to convenience, high-quality products, and cutting-edge technology.
- **What Sells**: Premium products, innovative tech gadgets,

luxury goods, and trendy fashion items perform well in urban markets. Urban consumers appreciate convenience, quality, and novelty, making them more receptive to international brands and new trends.

Rural Markets

- **Key Characteristics**: Rural areas in Japan are generally more conservative and traditional, with a focus on community values, local craftsmanship, and sustainability. Rural consumers tend to be loyal to trusted brands and often prefer goods that are locally produced or have a cultural connection.
- **What Sells**: Artisanal goods, traditional crafts, eco-friendly products, and local foods are popular in rural markets. Products that align with Japanese culture, sustainability, and community values tend to resonate well with rural consumers.

1.3 Understanding Japanese Consumer Culture

Japanese consumer culture is rooted in values of quality, aesthetics, and customer service. Japanese consumers are highly detail-oriented and expect exceptional quality and attention to detail in the products and services they purchase. Below are some of the key values that shape Japanese consumer behaviour.

Omotenashi – The Art of Hospitality

Omotenashi, or the spirit of hospitality, is deeply embedded in Japanese culture and extends to the customer experience. Japanese consumers expect brands to provide attentive, respectful, and meticulous service.

- **Key Insight**: Delivering excellent customer service, from pre-sale assistance to after-sales support, is crucial for success in Japan. Show attentiveness to customer needs and go the extra mile to demonstrate your commitment to service.

Quality and Craftsmanship

Japanese consumers are known for their preference for quality and craftsmanship. They are often willing to pay more for products that reflect a high level of precision, durability, and artistry.

- **Key Insight**: Emphasising quality and detailing the craftsmanship behind your products can enhance your brand's appeal. Japanese consumers appreciate brands that demonstrate a commitment to excellence, especially in fashion, technology, and artisanal goods.

Simplicity and Aesthetics

Simplicity, minimalism, and aesthetic beauty are highly valued in Japanese culture, influencing everything from fashion to home décor and product packaging.

- **Key Insight**: Invest in simple, elegant, and thoughtfully designed packaging that reflects Japanese aesthetic sensibilities. Avoid excessive designs or flashy elements; instead, focus on understated beauty and functionality.

Sustainability and Environmental Awareness

Sustainability has become an important consideration for many Japanese consumers, particularly younger ones. Products that incorporate eco-friendly materials, sustainable sourcing, or minimalistic packaging are increasingly popular.

- **Key Insight**: Brands that prioritise eco-friendly practices and sustainability are likely to resonate with Japanese consumers. Highlight any environmentally friendly aspects of your products, such as biodegradable packaging or ethically sourced materials.

Brand Loyalty and Trust

Japanese consumers are known for being brand-loyal but are selective when forming these loyalties. They tend to research products thoroughly and are highly influenced by reviews, recommendations, and a brand's reputation.

- **Key Insight**: Building a strong brand reputation in

Japan takes time but pays off in the form of loyal customers. Establish trust through consistent quality, transparency, and excellent customer service. Positive reviews and testimonials can significantly enhance your credibility in the Japanese market.

Chapter 1 - Summary

Japan's regions, urban-rural dynamics, and cultural values all shape consumer behaviour and expectations. From Tokyo's high-tech and trend-driven market to the traditional preferences in rural areas, Japan's consumer landscape is diverse yet united by shared values of quality, hospitality, and aesthetic appreciation. Understanding these nuances and tailoring your offerings accordingly will provide a solid foundation for entering the Japanese market. By aligning with Japanese values of quality, simplicity, and sustainability, your brand can establish a meaningful and successful presence in this unique and sophisticated market.

CHAPTER 2: THE LOGISTICS OFTRAVELLING IN JAPAN

Japan's advanced infrastructure, efficient public transport, and modern amenities make travelling across the country convenient and straightforward. Whether you're attending business meetings in Tokyo, setting up a market stall in Osaka, or exploring rural areas for potential distribution, Japan's transport systems and accommodations provide comfort, convenience, and reliability. This chapter covers essential travel logistics for business visitors, including transport options, accommodation recommendations, and tips for managing inventory and shipping within Japan.

2.1 Transportation Options

Japan's extensive transport network includes one of the world's most efficient rail systems, an array of domestic flights, and an organised public transport system that connects cities and towns across the country. Choosing the right mode of transportation can make travel both economical and productive.

Public Transport: Reliable and Comprehensive

Japan's public transport system is renowned for its punctuality, cleanliness, and extensive coverage. Most major cities have well-developed networks of trains, subways, and buses, making it easy to navigate urban areas.

- **Train System**: The **Japan Rail (JR)** system operates an extensive network of trains, including the Shinkansen (bullet train) for long-distance travel. Japan also has numerous private rail companies that operate within and between cities.
    - **Japan Rail Pass**: If you plan to travel between

cities frequently, consider purchasing a **Japan Rail Pass**. Available only to foreign visitors, the pass offers unlimited travel on JR trains, including the Shinkansen, for a set period.
- **Local Trains and Subways**: Most cities, including Tokyo, Osaka, and Kyoto, have comprehensive local train and subway networks. The **Suica** and **PASMO** cards are reloadable cards that can be used on public transport across Japan, simplifying travel.

- **Buses**: Buses are often the best option for reaching areas not covered by the rail network, especially in rural regions. Japan's long-distance buses are also a budget-friendly alternative for intercity travel.
  - **Convenience**: Buses are clean, punctual, and well-maintained. Some long-distance buses offer overnight routes, allowing travellers to save on accommodation while covering significant distances.

Shinkansen (Bullet Train): Fast and Efficient

The Shinkansen is a high-speed rail network connecting Japan's major cities. Known for its punctuality and comfort, the Shinkansen is ideal for business travellers needing quick and reliable transport.

- **Routes and Destinations**: The Shinkansen connects Tokyo with cities such as Osaka, Kyoto, Nagoya, and Fukuoka. With speeds of up to 320 km/h, it's an efficient way to travel long distances.
- **Booking Tickets**: Tickets can be booked online, at train stations, or through travel agents. The Japan Rail Pass offers unlimited Shinkansen travel on eligible routes, making it a cost-effective option for multiple journeys.

Domestic Flights

For long-distance travel or trips to more remote locations, such as Okinawa or Hokkaido, domestic flights are a practical option. Japan has several budget airlines, including **Peach Aviation**,

Jetstar Japan, and **Skymark**, that offer affordable flights between major cities.

- **Convenience**: Domestic flights are frequent, reliable, and efficient, with short check-in times. Major airports, such as Haneda, Narita, and Kansai International, connect Japan's main islands and key business locations.
- **Regional Airports**: Many cities have regional airports, which can make travel to smaller cities and towns more convenient. Regional flights are available, especially to popular tourist destinations and areas with limited rail connections.

Car Rentals

While Japan's public transport system generally makes car rentals unnecessary, they can be beneficial when travelling to rural areas or locations with limited public transport options.

- **Requirements**: Foreign visitors need an **International Driving Permit (IDP)** along with their national driving licence to rent a car in Japan. Some rental agencies offer navigation systems in English, which can be helpful for non-Japanese speakers.
- **Traffic and Navigation**: Traffic in major cities can be congested, and parking is often expensive and limited. However, rural areas offer easier navigation, making car rentals a good choice for countryside travel.

2.2 Accommodation for Business Travellers

Japan offers a range of accommodation options, from business hotels designed for professionals to traditional inns and modern serviced apartments. Choosing the right accommodation can enhance productivity and comfort during your stay.

Business Hotels

Business hotels are widely available in Japan's urban centres and are designed to meet the needs of business travellers. These hotels are typically economical and equipped with essential amenities such as free Wi-Fi, work desks, and business centres.

- **Examples**: Chains like **APA Hotel**, **Toyoko Inn**, and **Daiwa Roynet** have locations in multiple cities, providing a consistent and convenient experience for business travellers.
- **Key Areas**: In Tokyo, popular business districts such as **Shinjuku**, **Shibuya**, and **Tokyo Station** area offer numerous business hotel options. Osaka's **Umeda** and **Namba** areas are also ideal for business stays.

Traditional Inns (Ryokan)

For a unique experience, consider staying at a **ryokan** (traditional Japanese inn), which provides an immersive cultural experience with tatami-matted rooms, communal baths, and traditional Japanese meals. While ryokan are less common for business stays, they are popular in regions known for their natural beauty, such as Hakone and Kyoto.

- **Benefits**: Staying at a ryokan can provide insight into Japanese culture and offers a relaxing experience, especially useful for building client relationships or entertaining business partners.
- **Booking**: Ryokan can be booked through popular travel sites or directly with the inn. Note that some ryokan may not offer amenities such as Wi-Fi, so check in advance if you require connectivity for work.

Serviced Apartments

Serviced apartments are ideal for longer stays or if you need more space. They often include kitchen facilities, laundry, and other amenities, providing more flexibility than traditional hotels.

- **Examples**: Providers like **Oakwood Premier** and **Ascott Marunouchi Tokyo** offer serviced apartments in major cities with full amenities, including workspaces, fitness centres, and dining options.

- **Best For**: Long-term business stays, families, or travellers who need more space for work or meetings.

2.3 Organising the Transport of Goods

Efficient and reliable logistics are essential for businesses transporting goods or managing inventory in Japan. Japan has an advanced domestic shipping network, with options ranging from postal services to private couriers.

Japan Post

Japan Post is the national postal service and offers reliable and cost-effective shipping solutions for domestic deliveries. It's an ideal choice for smaller items or regular business shipping needs.

- **Delivery Options**: Japan Post offers various services, including express delivery (EMS), standard parcels, and international shipping. Their service is known for punctuality and reliability, making it suitable for small-to-medium shipments.
- **Konbini Pick-Up**: Japan's convenience stores, known as **konbini**, offer pick-up and drop-off services for parcels. Major chains like **7-Eleven** and **Lawson** provide these services, making it convenient for customers and suppliers to access parcels at flexible times.

Private Couriers

Companies like **Yamato Transport (Kuroneko)** and **Sagawa Express** are popular for their prompt and efficient courier services across Japan. These couriers offer reliable delivery options, including same-day and next-day services.

- **Advantages**: Private couriers provide additional services, such as refrigerated delivery for perishable items and large package handling. Their extensive networks make them ideal for businesses with high-volume shipping needs.
- **Click-and-Collect Options**: Many private couriers offer

click-and-collect services at convenience stores and lockers, which are increasingly popular among urban consumers for flexibility and convenience.

International Shipping

If you're importing goods into Japan, understanding customs requirements and choosing the right shipping partner is essential. Japan has strict regulations for imports, so ensure you have the necessary documentation and permits.

- **Customs and Import Duties**: Japan has detailed customs requirements, and certain goods may require permits or certificates. Working with a customs broker can help streamline the process.

- **Shipping Partners**: Companies like **FedEx**, **DHL**, and **UPS** have strong networks in Japan, providing reliable international shipping options with customs assistance. For regular shipments, consider a partnership with a preferred shipping provider to negotiate rates and streamline logistics.

Chapter 2 - Summary

Japan's world-class transport and logistics infrastructure makes it easy to travel between cities, manage inventory, and deliver products to customers efficiently. Whether you're navigating Tokyo's subway system, travelling on the Shinkansen, or organising deliveries through private couriers, Japan offers a range of reliable and efficient options for business travellers. By planning your accommodation and logistics carefully, you can ensure that your time in Japan is productive and well-organised, setting you up for success in this dynamic and demanding market.

CHAPTER 3: SETTING UP YOUR BUSINESS IN JAPAN

Establishing a business in Japan involves careful planning and a clear understanding of the country's legal and regulatory environment. Japan offers a range of business structures suited to different needs, from small enterprises to larger corporations, each with its own tax and administrative obligations. This chapter provides a step-by-step guide to setting up a business in Japan, including selecting the appropriate business structure, managing taxes, and complying with Japanese consumer protection laws.

3.1 Choosing Your Business Structure

Selecting the right business structure is crucial for defining your legal obligations, tax liabilities, and the administrative responsibilities of your business in Japan. Japan offers several types of business structures for foreign entrepreneurs and companies.

Sole Proprietorship (Kojin Jigyo)

A **sole proprietorship** is a simple structure, suitable for small businesses and individual entrepreneurs. This structure requires minimal administrative requirements but involves personal liability for the business's debts and obligations.

- **Advantages**: Simple registration, minimal paperwork, and full control over business operations.
- **Disadvantages**: Personal liability, meaning your personal assets are at risk if the business incurs debt or legal obligations.
- **Registration**: Registering as a sole proprietor requires visiting your local **Tax Office** to complete tax

registration. You'll also need a **business registration certificate**, which is necessary for operating legally in Japan.

Godo Kaisha (GK) – Limited Liability Company

A **Godo Kaisha (GK)** is a popular option for small to medium-sized businesses. It offers limited liability, meaning your personal assets are protected, and provides more flexibility than other corporate structures.

- **Advantages**: Limited liability, flexible management structure, and lower administrative costs compared to a **Kabushiki Kaisha (KK)**.
- **Disadvantages**: Perceived as less prestigious than a KK, which may affect business credibility with certain partners or clients.
- **Registration**: Registering a GK involves submitting the **Articles of Incorporation** and other required documents to the Legal Affairs Bureau. The process typically takes a few weeks, and you'll need to pay a registration fee.

Kabushiki Kaisha (KK) – Corporation

A **Kabushiki Kaisha (KK)** is a corporation structure ideal for businesses planning to operate on a larger scale or seeking significant capital investment. KKs are considered highly credible in Japan and are often preferred by large corporations.

- **Advantages**: Limited liability, access to capital through issuing shares, and strong business credibility.
- **Disadvantages**: Higher administrative costs, more complex registration, and additional compliance requirements.
- **Registration**: Registering a KK involves drafting and submitting the Articles of Incorporation and appointing at least one director. Registration is handled by the Legal Affairs Bureau and requires a fee. A KK is subject to more

rigorous reporting and compliance requirements than a GK.

Branch Office or Representative Office

For foreign companies looking to enter the Japanese market without establishing a full-fledged subsidiary, setting up a **branch office** or **representative office** is an option. A branch office can conduct business transactions in Japan, while a representative office is limited to market research and support activities.

- **Branch Office**: Suitable for businesses planning to conduct transactions directly in Japan. Requires registration with the Legal Affairs Bureau and has similar tax obligations to Japanese companies.
- **Representative Office**: Ideal for conducting market research or supporting overseas business activities. It does not require registration with the Legal Affairs Bureau but is limited to non-commercial functions.

3.2 Managing Taxes and Consumption Tax (VAT)

Understanding Japan's tax system is essential for compliance and efficient financial planning. Japan's tax regime includes corporate tax, consumption tax (similar to VAT), and income tax, managed by the **National Tax Agency (NTA)**.

Corporate Tax

Corporate tax is levied on all companies operating in Japan, with rates that vary based on annual income and company size.

- **Rates (as of 2024)**:
    - **15%** on income up to JPY 8 million for smaller companies.
    - **23.2%** on income above JPY 8 million for larger companies.

Corporate tax returns must be filed annually, and accurate record-keeping of all business transactions is crucial for accurate tax reporting.

Consumption Tax (Shouhi-zei)

Consumption tax, Japan's equivalent to VAT, applies to most goods and services, with a standard rate of **10%**. Businesses with annual sales above JPY 10 million must register for consumption tax.

- **Registration**: Consumption tax registration can be completed through your local Tax Office. Businesses that qualify are required to charge consumption tax on taxable sales and submit quarterly or annual returns to the NTA.
- **Exemptions**: Certain products, such as food and beverages (excluding alcohol), are taxed at a reduced rate of 8%.

Withholding Tax

Withholding tax applies to payments made to foreign entities or individuals. If you are receiving income from a Japanese entity, they may withhold tax on the payment, with rates varying by income type and whether a tax treaty applies.

- **Types of Income**: Royalties, interest, and dividends are commonly subject to withholding tax, often at rates between 10-20%.
- **Tax Treaties**: Japan has tax treaties with many countries to reduce withholding tax rates. Check whether a treaty applies to your income to avoid double taxation.

3.3 Understanding Japanese Consumer Protection Laws

Japan has strict consumer protection laws, designed to ensure that consumers receive high-quality products and fair treatment. Compliance with these regulations is essential, particularly if you sell directly to Japanese consumers (B2C).

Product Safety Standards

Japan enforces strict safety standards for a variety of goods, including electronics, cosmetics, and food products. Products must meet these standards before they can be legally sold in Japan.

- **PSE Mark**: Electrical products must bear the **PSE Mark**, which certifies compliance with Japan's Electrical Appliance and Material Safety Law.
- **PSC Mark**: Certain consumer goods, such as lighters and helmets, require the **PSC Mark** to demonstrate compliance with the Consumer Product Safety Act.

Labelling Requirements

Japan has detailed labelling requirements for products, particularly in categories like food, cosmetics, and pharmaceuticals. Labels must be clear, accurate, and in Japanese to comply with local laws.

- **Required Information**: Labelling for food and cosmetics should include ingredients, allergens, usage instructions, and shelf life. Clear labelling helps build trust with Japanese consumers and ensures compliance.
- **Localisation**: Ensure all product labelling, instructions, and marketing materials are available in Japanese. Compliance with labelling regulations is particularly crucial for businesses in food, cosmetics, and pharmaceutical sectors.

Data Protection (APPI)

Japan's **Act on the Protection of Personal Information (APPI)** governs how businesses collect, store, and use personal data. Compliance with APPI is mandatory for any business that handles customer data.

- **Privacy Policy**: Publish a clear privacy policy outlining how personal data is collected, used, and stored. Customers have the right to request information about their data usage and to demand deletion of their data under certain conditions.
- **Data Security**: Ensure robust security measures are in place to protect personal data from unauthorised access. Non-compliance with APPI can lead to penalties and

impact customer trust.

Right to Return and Refund Policies

Japanese consumers have the right to return certain goods within specified timeframes. While the rules vary by industry, offering a transparent returns policy can enhance customer confidence and brand reputation.

- **Returns Policy**: Ensure that your returns policy is clearly stated, especially for e-commerce or direct-to-consumer sales. Most retailers offer at least seven days for returns, though timeframes vary based on the product category.
- **Customer Service**: Japanese consumers expect responsive and respectful customer service. Efficient handling of returns and refunds is essential for maintaining a positive reputation.

Chapter 3 - Summary

Setting up a business in Japan involves choosing the appropriate business structure, understanding tax obligations, and adhering to Japan's consumer protection laws. Whether you opt for a sole proprietorship, a GK, or a KK, each structure comes with unique requirements and benefits. Japan's consumer protection regulations are strict, with a strong emphasis on product safety, data security, and fair treatment of customers. Adhering to these regulations and consistently delivering quality will help build credibility and trust in Japan's discerning market.

CHAPTER 4: WHAT TO SELL IN JAPAN: MARKET INSIGHTS

Japan's consumer market is unique, with a strong emphasis on quality, detail, and service. Japanese consumers are known for being discerning, brand-loyal, and highly receptive to products that embody quality, innovation, and aesthetics. This chapter explores popular product categories, insights into seasonal and regional trends, and the growing demand for sustainable and ethically sourced goods in Japan.

4.1 Best-Selling Product Categories

Japanese consumers appreciate products that reflect quality craftsmanship, innovation, and aesthetic appeal. The following product categories have consistently strong demand, with opportunities for new brands that can meet these expectations.

Beauty and Skincare

Japan is one of the world's largest beauty markets, with a preference for high-quality skincare and cosmetics. Japanese consumers favour products that prioritise skin health, natural ingredients, and minimalism in design.

- **What Sells**: Skincare items like cleansers, serums, lotions, and sunscreens are popular, with a focus on anti-ageing and moisturising properties. Japanese consumers also appreciate natural and hypoallergenic ingredients.
- **Trends**: Eco-friendly beauty, cruelty-free, and organic skincare products are on the rise. Minimalist packaging and natural aesthetics resonate well with Japanese consumers, as does the growing popularity of "clean

beauty" products.

Fashion and Apparel

Japanese fashion is distinctive, with a reputation for balancing traditional styles with contemporary trends. Japanese consumers are known for their attention to detail, valuing quality fabrics, and well-constructed garments.

- **What Sells**: Minimalist and high-quality clothing, streetwear, and accessories such as handbags, jewellery, and footwear are highly sought after. Unique, niche fashion brands are popular, especially among younger demographics.
- **Trends**: Sustainable fashion is gaining traction, particularly among younger consumers. Brands that highlight their ethical production processes, eco-friendly materials, or support for traditional craftsmanship have a strong appeal.

Tech and Gadgets

Japan has a high demand for tech gadgets, especially those that enhance convenience, entertainment, or home automation. Japanese consumers are quick to adopt new technology and prefer products that combine quality with functionality.

- **What Sells**: Smartphones, wearables like smartwatches, headphones, gaming consoles, and home automation devices such as smart speakers are popular. Japanese consumers often seek gadgets that integrate seamlessly into daily life.
- **Trends**: Smart home devices and IoT (Internet of Things) products are increasingly popular, as are devices that support health and wellbeing, such as fitness trackers and sleep monitors.

Gourmet Food and Beverages

Japan has a rich food culture, and consumers are interested in gourmet, health-conscious, and unique international foods.

There's also a trend towards products that are visually appealing and shareable on social media.

- **What Sells**: Artisanal snacks, premium teas and coffees, organic and health-focused foods, and international delicacies are well-received. Items such as matcha, specialty chocolates, and local delicacies have strong appeal.
- **Trends**: Japanese consumers are increasingly interested in products that promote health and wellness, such as low-sugar, low-fat, and organic options. The presentation is also essential, with attractive, minimalist packaging adding value to gourmet foods.

Home and Lifestyle Products

As Japanese consumers spend more time at home, there has been a growing interest in products that enhance the home environment. Minimalism and aesthetics are highly valued in home décor and lifestyle products.

- **What Sells**: Home décor items, furniture, kitchenware, and organisation solutions are popular. Products that promote relaxation, such as candles, diffusers, and home spa items, are also in demand.
- **Trends**: Japanese consumers are drawn to minimalist, space-saving designs. Eco-friendly and sustainably sourced home products are particularly popular, especially among urban dwellers with limited space.

4.2 Seasonal and Regional Trends

Japan's culture is deeply connected to its seasonal and regional traditions, with consumer demand fluctuating around festivals and holidays. Understanding these patterns can help you tailor your product offerings to meet the changing preferences of Japanese consumers.

Seasonal Trends

- **New Year (Shogatsu)**: Celebrated in January, New Year is one of Japan's most significant holidays, with gift-giving as a common practice. Products like high-quality food items, skincare, and home goods make excellent gifts, as well as traditional New Year decorations.

- **Cherry Blossom Season (Hanami)**: Cherry blossom season, typically in March and April, is a time for gatherings and picnics under the blossoms. Items like portable food, picnic accessories, and seasonal-themed products (such as sakura-flavoured snacks and drinks) are in high demand.

- **Summer and Obon Festival**: Summer is a festival season in Japan, and Obon (in August) is a time for family gatherings and traditional festivities. Lightweight clothing, cooling gadgets, and seasonal foods like ice cream and fruit-flavoured drinks sell well during this period.

- **Winter and Christmas**: While not traditionally celebrated, Christmas has become a popular time for shopping, especially for gifts. Festive items, winter apparel, and luxury goods see a surge in demand in December.

Regional Trends

- **Tokyo**: As Japan's economic hub, Tokyo's market is diverse and trend-driven. Consumers in Tokyo tend to favour high-end, innovative products and are more likely to adopt international trends quickly.

- **Osaka**: Known for its food culture, Osaka consumers appreciate products that offer value and quality. Osaka is a suitable market for reasonably priced goods, unique food products, and everyday essentials.

- **Kyoto**: Kyoto has a more traditional, artisanal culture, with a preference for products that reflect Japanese heritage, such as crafts, tea, and natural skincare.

- **Okinawa**: The subtropical climate and unique local culture of Okinawa make it a niche market. Products related to wellness, outdoor activities, and eco-tourism appeal to both locals and tourists.

4.3 Sustainability and Ethical Products

Sustainability is gaining importance in Japan, with consumers—particularly younger ones—showing a preference for brands that demonstrate environmental responsibility. Products that incorporate eco-friendly materials, sustainable production processes, and ethical sourcing are increasingly popular.

Eco-Friendly Products

Products that prioritise eco-friendly packaging, minimal waste, and renewable materials resonate well with Japanese consumers, who appreciate efforts toward sustainability.

- **What Sells**: Reusable items (such as water bottles and shopping bags), biodegradable packaging, and products that reduce environmental impact. Japanese consumers are also receptive to minimalistic packaging and brands that avoid unnecessary plastic or non-recyclable materials.

Ethically Sourced Goods

Many Japanese consumers appreciate products that are ethically sourced, supporting fair trade and environmentally conscious practices. This trend is particularly strong in food, fashion, and beauty.

- **What Sells**: Fair-trade food products, clothing made from organic or recycled materials, and goods that benefit social or environmental causes. Transparent labelling about sourcing and ethical practices builds consumer trust and loyalty.

Local and Artisanal Products

There is a growing appreciation for locally made and artisanal products that reflect craftsmanship and cultural heritage. Japanese consumers value items that showcase traditional methods, high quality, and a sense of authenticity.

- **What Sells**: Handmade crafts, locally produced foods, and products that highlight Japanese craftsmanship, such as ceramics, textiles, and paper goods. Artisanal goods that blend traditional aesthetics with contemporary function appeal to both Japanese and international consumers.

Chapter 4 - Summary

The Japanese market offers vast opportunities across various product categories. From high-quality skincare and fashion to innovative tech gadgets and gourmet foods, Japanese consumers value products that align with their cultural preferences for quality, aesthetics, and ethical production. By understanding seasonal and regional trends, you can adapt your offerings to meet changing consumer demands. The growing interest in sustainability further enhances opportunities for brands that prioritise eco-friendly practices and ethically sourced goods. With these insights, your brand can appeal to Japan's discerning market and build a strong customer base.

CHAPTER 5: SELLING INDUSTRIAL PRODUCTS AND SERVICES IN JAPAN

Japan is known for its advanced industrial sector, driven by its automotive, electronics, robotics, and machinery industries. As one of the world's leading industrial economies, Japan prioritises quality, innovation, and precision in its manufacturing processes. Selling industrial products and services in Japan requires a deep understanding of the local market demands, regulatory landscape, and business culture. This chapter offers insights into Japan's industrial market, effective market entry strategies, and approaches for building partnerships with Japanese businesses.

5.1 Understanding the Japanese Industrial Market

Japan's industrial market is diverse, technologically advanced, and highly competitive. Known for its emphasis on quality, Japanese industries prioritise products that enhance productivity, reliability, and precision.

Key Sectors for Industrial Products

- **Automotive**: Japan is home to global automotive giants like Toyota, Honda, and Nissan, with a constant demand for high-quality machinery, robotics, and automotive components that optimise production and meet strict environmental standards.

- **Electronics and Semiconductors**: Japan is a world leader in electronics, requiring precision equipment, cleanroom technologies, and advanced manufacturing tools to support companies like Sony, Panasonic, and Toshiba.

- **Robotics and Automation**: Japan is at the forefront of industrial robotics, making it one of the top markets for high-tech machinery, AI-driven solutions, and automated assembly tools.
- **Aerospace and Defence**: Japan's aerospace industry is expanding, with increasing demand for high-precision components, advanced materials, and sustainable technologies that meet rigorous industry standards.

Focus on Quality, Innovation, and Precision

Japanese companies prioritise products that embody precision, reliability, and technical excellence. Innovation is highly valued, especially if it provides tangible improvements in efficiency, sustainability, or quality.

- **Quality Assurance**: Japan's high standards mean that products must meet rigorous quality criteria. Certifications like ISO and CE are essential for gaining credibility.
- **Technological Innovation**: Japanese firms are forward-thinking and appreciate advanced technologies. Products that feature IoT integration, AI capabilities, or data analytics have strong appeal.
- **Sustainability**: With a focus on sustainable practices, Japan's industrial sector increasingly demands eco-friendly machinery and energy-efficient equipment. Emphasising sustainability in your product offerings will likely resonate well in this market.

5.2 Market Entry Strategies for Industrial Products and Services

Entering Japan's industrial market requires a well-thought-out approach. Building a credible presence, establishing partnerships, and localising your products to meet industry-specific demands are crucial for success.

Establishing Local Partnerships

Collaborating with local distributors, agents, or suppliers is essential in Japan's industrial sector. A local partner can help navigate complex regulations, provide market insights, and facilitate network building.

- **Choosing the Right Partner**: Look for partners with extensive experience, a solid reputation, and technical expertise in your industry. Distributors familiar with your field can offer valuable insights and improve product credibility.
- **Joint Ventures and Strategic Alliances**: Forming joint ventures or strategic alliances with Japanese companies can provide access to local resources, expertise, and networks. This approach is particularly beneficial for businesses with limited experience in the Japanese market.

Localising Marketing and Technical Documentation

Japanese professionals value detailed and accurate information, so localising your marketing materials, technical documentation, and support resources is essential.

- **Technical Documentation**: Translate manuals, technical specifications, and safety information into Japanese. Clear, accurate documentation demonstrates professionalism and helps comply with local safety standards.
- **Website Localisation**: Developing a Japanese-language website, or a dedicated Japanese section, is essential. Many Japanese companies research potential suppliers online, so a well-presented, localised website will enhance credibility and accessibility.

Attending Industry Events and Trade Shows

Japan's industrial trade shows and conferences offer excellent opportunities to showcase your products, meet potential clients, and establish a presence in the Japanese market. Events like the **International Robot Exhibition (iREX)** and **Manufacturing**

World Japan attract industrial professionals from across the country.

- **Networking**: Trade shows allow you to network with prospective customers, distributors, and suppliers. Networking is often the first step to building long-term business relationships in Japan.
- **Product Demonstrations**: Demonstrating your product's functionality and benefits in a live setting can attract Japanese buyers who value technical detail and hands-on experience with new technology.

5.3 Compliance and Regulatory Considerations

Japan has strict regulations regarding quality, safety, and environmental impact, particularly in industrial sectors. Familiarising yourself with the regulatory landscape is essential for ensuring your products meet Japanese standards and for avoiding compliance issues.

Product Safety Standards and Certifications

Many industrial products must meet Japan's stringent safety standards, which may include third-party certifications and inspections.

- **PSE Mark**: Electrical products must carry the **PSE Mark** to demonstrate compliance with Japan's Electrical Appliance and Material Safety Law.
- **Other Certifications**: ISO certifications, especially ISO 9001 and ISO 14001, are valued by Japanese companies as indicators of quality and environmental responsibility. Japanese businesses often seek these certifications when evaluating suppliers.

Import Regulations and Tariffs

Understanding Japan's import regulations, tariffs, and duty requirements is critical when entering the market.

- **Customs Documentation**: Ensure that all necessary

import documents are in order, including certificates of origin, invoices, and product specifications. Customs clearance can be expedited by providing accurate documentation and adhering to Japanese regulations.

- **Duty-Free Opportunities**: Certain products may qualify for reduced or duty-free import under the Japan-United Kingdom Free Trade Agreement. Check whether your products are eligible for these benefits.

Environmental Regulations

Japan's commitment to sustainability is reflected in its environmental regulations, which have become stricter in recent years. Japanese companies often seek eco-friendly suppliers to align with sustainability goals.

- **Eco-Friendly Certifications**: Products with eco-friendly certifications, such as ISO 14001 for environmental management, may have a competitive advantage.
- **Recycling and Waste Management Requirements**: Some industries, such as electronics and automotive, require suppliers to adhere to waste management and recycling guidelines. Compliance with these regulations can make your products more attractive to Japanese firms.

5.4 Building Relationships and Sales Channels

Establishing a strong network and understanding Japanese business practices are crucial for building successful sales channels in Japan. Japanese companies highly value trust, reliability, and long-term relationships, so investing time and effort in relationship-building is essential.

Establishing Trust and Credibility

Credibility is a key factor in the Japanese industrial market, as buyers seek suppliers they can depend on for quality and consistency.

- **Quality Guarantees**: Offering warranties, after-sales support, or quality guarantees can help establish trust. Japanese companies prefer suppliers who can demonstrate a commitment to long-term product support and maintenance.

- **Customer Testimonials and Case Studies**: Sharing case studies, testimonials, and references from reputable clients will enhance your credibility. Japanese buyers value proven performance and tend to trust products with a track record of success.

Developing a Dedicated Sales Team or Local Office

Having a local presence, such as a sales team or office, can improve your ability to manage client relationships, oversee sales activities, and respond to customer inquiries quickly.

- **Sales Engineers and Technical Support**: Employing knowledgeable sales engineers or technical support staff who understand your product's specifications will benefit your business. Japanese buyers value knowledgeable representatives who can answer detailed questions.

- **Local Office Advantages**: Establishing a local office shows your commitment to the Japanese market. It allows you to handle logistics more effectively, comply with regulations, and provide prompt customer service.

Offering After-Sales Support and Maintenance

Providing after-sales support and maintenance is essential for building a loyal customer base in Japan's industrial market. Japanese companies value suppliers who offer reliable maintenance services and quick issue resolution.

- **Training and Maintenance Packages**: Offering training for clients' staff on equipment use and maintenance can set you apart from competitors. Maintenance packages and service contracts also appeal to Japanese buyers seeking long-term reliability.

- **Spare Parts and Repair Services**: The availability of spare parts and repair services is often a deciding factor for Japanese companies. Establishing a local inventory of spare parts or a repair centre can improve customer satisfaction and reinforce your reputation for reliability.

Chapter 5 - Summary

Selling industrial products and services in Japan's competitive, high-standard market requires a deep understanding of local demands, regulatory compliance, and a commitment to quality and innovation. By establishing local partnerships, attending industry events, and ensuring regulatory compliance, you can successfully navigate the Japanese market. Building trust through quality assurance, after-sales support, and localised marketing will help you establish long-term relationships with Japanese companies and unlock significant opportunities for growth in this advanced industrial market.

CHAPTER 6: SELLING AT MARKETS AND FAIRS IN JAPAN

Japan's vibrant market and fair culture provides an excellent opportunity for businesses to reach consumers directly, showcase products, and engage with a diverse audience. From bustling city markets to seasonal fairs and festivals, Japan's markets attract both locals and tourists looking for unique, high-quality, and often artisanal goods. In this chapter, we'll explore some of Japan's most popular markets, tips for setting up an inviting stall, and strategies for connecting with Japanese consumers effectively.

6.1 Famous Markets in Japan

Each major city in Japan hosts well-known markets that attract thousands of visitors daily, offering an excellent platform for businesses selling unique products, food items, and traditional goods. Below are some of Japan's most iconic markets.

Tsukiji Outer Market (Tokyo)

- **Overview**: Known worldwide for its seafood, Tsukiji Market also offers a variety of Japanese food products, kitchen tools, and artisanal items. It's a popular spot for both locals and tourists seeking high-quality foods and unique kitchenware.
- **What Sells**: Fresh produce, seafood, speciality Japanese food items (like miso and soy sauce), and kitchenware. This market is particularly suitable for vendors offering premium food items, artisanal sauces, and unique cooking tools.

Nishiki Market (Kyoto)

- **Overview**: Often called "Kyoto's Kitchen," Nishiki

Market is a narrow, bustling street lined with shops selling local delicacies, fresh produce, and traditional handicrafts. It's popular among tourists and locals alike.

- **What Sells**: Traditional Kyoto foods (such as tsukemono pickles), tea, ceramics, and souvenirs. Vendors selling artisanal goods, food products, or handmade crafts will find Nishiki Market a great place to connect with consumers who appreciate Japanese heritage.

Ameya-Yokocho (Tokyo)

- **Overview**: This bustling market street in Ueno is known for its affordable prices, variety of goods, and vibrant atmosphere. Ameya-Yokocho is popular among bargain hunters and tourists.
- **What Sells**: Fashion, cosmetics, food items, and everyday goods. It's ideal for vendors with trendy, affordable products or unique items not easily found in typical Japanese stores.

Osaka Tenjinbashi-suji Shopping Street (Osaka)

- **Overview**: Known as Japan's longest shopping street, Tenjinbashi-suji stretches over 2.6 kilometres and features a wide range of shops selling everything from clothing to household goods.
- **What Sells**: Fashion, accessories, traditional crafts, and everyday goods. This location is great for vendors selling fashion, household items, and small gifts.

Okinawa Heiwa Dori Shopping Street (Naha, Okinawa)

- **Overview**: Located in Okinawa, this market street is known for its traditional Okinawan crafts, local foods, and souvenirs. It's popular with both locals and visitors interested in Okinawa's unique culture.
- **What Sells**: Handcrafted textiles, ceramics, traditional snacks, and unique Okinawan souvenirs. Vendors offering artisanal or culturally specific goods will find a

receptive audience here.

6.2 Setting Up Your Stall

Creating an attractive, welcoming, and well-organised stall is essential for drawing customers in Japan's competitive market environments. Japanese consumers appreciate attention to detail, so a carefully crafted setup can make a significant difference.

Stall Design and Layout

- **Open and Accessible Layout**: Arrange your products so they are easy to browse, avoiding clutter. Place your most eye-catching products at the front to draw people in, and create clear paths within the stall for customers to navigate comfortably.

- **Use Vertical Space**: Use shelving, risers, or stands to add layers and dimension to your display. Japanese consumers are accustomed to organised displays, so creating visual interest without overcrowding your stall is key.

- **Clear Signage and Pricing**: Ensure that your stall has clear signage in Japanese, and clearly display prices for each item. Price transparency is appreciated in Japan, and clear labels make browsing more convenient for customers.

Aesthetics and Décor

- **Simple and Elegant Decor**: Minimalistic and tasteful decor resonates well with Japanese consumers. Avoid overly bright colours or complex displays; instead, focus on natural materials, subtle decorations, and a clean layout that highlights your products.

- **Cultural Touches**: If your products are connected to Japanese culture or traditions, incorporate small cultural elements such as washi paper (Japanese paper) or subtle floral accents in your décor to reflect this.

Packaging and Presentation

- **Quality Packaging**: Japanese consumers highly value presentation and packaging. Use quality materials, eco-friendly options, and a minimalist design that reflects the quality of your product.
- **Gift-Wrapping Services**: Offering gift-wrapping services can set you apart, especially for markets frequented by tourists or during holiday seasons. Japanese customers often purchase market items as gifts, so thoughtful packaging adds appeal.

6.3 Connecting with Japanese Customers

Interacting with customers in a respectful, friendly, and attentive manner is essential for building a positive reputation and fostering customer loyalty in Japan. Japanese consumers value service and politeness, so customer interactions should be genuine and professional.

Politeness and Respect

- **Greet Customers Politely**: A simple greeting like "Irasshaimase" (welcome) is customary and signals your attentiveness. When engaging in conversation, be polite, listen attentively, and maintain a positive demeanour.
- **Avoid Hard Selling**: Japanese consumers often prefer to browse without feeling pressured, so allow them to explore your products freely. Be available to answer questions and provide assistance but avoid overly aggressive sales tactics.

Telling Your Product's Story

- **Share Product Details**: Japanese customers appreciate knowing the background of a product, including its materials, craftsmanship, and inspiration. Briefly explain these details, highlighting any unique or authentic aspects that add value.

- **Use Japanese When Possible**: Even a basic level of Japanese or a few key phrases can make a positive impression. If you're unable to speak Japanese, consider using bilingual signage and materials, which can bridge the language gap and convey professionalism.

Encouraging Sales and Repeat Business

- **Special Deals and Bundles**: Offering bundle deals or small discounts for multiple purchases can encourage customers to buy more. Bundling complementary items together, like a tea set with loose-leaf tea, can add value.

- **Provide Business Cards or Flyers**: Including a business card, flyer, or small promotional material with each purchase can help customers remember your brand and encourage future visits or referrals. Ensure contact information and social media details are included, especially if you have an online store.

6.4 Navigating Market Regulations and Costs

Before setting up a stall at a market or fair, it's essential to familiarise yourself with local regulations, fees, and any required permits. These requirements can vary by location and market type, so it's best to confirm details with market organisers well in advance.

Applying for a Stall

- **Application Process**: Many popular markets require vendors to apply in advance. Applications are usually reviewed to ensure products align with the market's theme or standards, particularly in craft or food markets. Check the market's website or contact organisers to learn about application deadlines and required documents.

- **Permits and Certifications**: Food vendors often require additional permits or certifications, especially when selling perishable items. Make sure to comply with any health and safety requirements set by local authorities or the market management.

Stall Fees

- **Renting a Stall**: Stall fees vary depending on the location, popularity, and size of the market. Major urban markets, such as those in Tokyo or Kyoto, may have higher fees, while smaller or regional markets tend to be more affordable.
- **Revenue Sharing**: Some markets, especially larger ones, may require a percentage of revenue as part of the stall fee arrangement. It's important to understand the cost structure in advance to budget accordingly.

Insurance and Liability

- **Public Liability Insurance**: Some markets require vendors to have public liability insurance, covering potential incidents related to the stall or products. While it's not always mandatory, insurance is recommended for added protection and peace of mind.
- **Product Liability**: If you're selling consumable products, such as food or skincare, product liability insurance is advisable to protect against claims related to product safety or health concerns.

Chapter 6 - Summary

Selling at markets and fairs in Japan is a rewarding opportunity to connect directly with consumers, build brand awareness, and showcase products in a dynamic setting. By setting up a well-organised and visually appealing stall, engaging respectfully with customers, and offering thoughtful packaging, you can create a memorable experience that encourages sales and builds a positive reputation. Navigating local regulations and understanding the unique preferences of Japanese consumers will further enhance your success in Japan's vibrant market scene.

CHAPTER 7: SELLING ONLINE IN JAPAN

Japan's e-commerce market is highly developed and continues to grow, with a tech-savvy consumer base that increasingly prefers online shopping for convenience and variety. Selling online in Japan provides businesses with opportunities to reach a broad audience and build brand visibility. In this chapter, we'll cover the key e-commerce platforms, strategies for creating a localised digital presence, and essential considerations for providing secure payment options and efficient shipping.

7.1 Popular E-Commerce Platforms in Japan

Selecting the right platform is essential for gaining traction in Japan's competitive online market. Japan has several popular e-commerce platforms, each catering to different product types and consumer preferences.

Rakuten

Rakuten is one of Japan's largest and most established e-commerce platforms, often referred to as the "Amazon of Japan." It offers an extensive range of products and includes loyalty programmes and rewards that Japanese consumers highly value.

- **Advantages**: Rakuten has a broad customer base and offers marketing support, loyalty points, and visibility through Rakuten's ecosystem of services.
- **Best For**: Fashion, beauty products, electronics, household goods, and food items. Rakuten's points system makes it popular with consumers looking for value and rewards on purchases.

Amazon Japan

Amazon Japan is a leading platform, known for fast delivery options and a wide range of products. With its high trustworthiness and reliability, Amazon Japan is ideal for businesses looking to attract a large, loyal customer base.

- **Advantages**: Amazon Japan's well-established delivery network (including Amazon Prime) is highly appealing to Japanese consumers who value fast, reliable shipping.
- **Best For**: Consumer electronics, books, everyday essentials, and items that benefit from quick delivery. Amazon's robust fulfilment services and brand reputation make it ideal for companies seeking broad reach.

Yahoo! Shopping

Yahoo! Shopping is a popular platform in Japan, backed by SoftBank and a favourite among price-conscious consumers. It's known for offering competitive pricing and regular deals, attracting a loyal customer base.

- **Advantages**: Yahoo! Shopping's integrated promotions and deals attract customers seeking value, and its connection with SoftBank provides extensive reach.
- **Best For**: Apparel, electronics, cosmetics, and products targeting price-sensitive consumers. Yahoo! Shopping is especially effective for discounted and competitively priced items.

Mercari

Mercari is Japan's top online marketplace for second-hand and unique items. Known as a peer-to-peer platform, Mercari attracts consumers looking for budget-friendly or hard-to-find goods.

- **Advantages**: Mercari's user-friendly platform and diverse product offerings make it popular with younger consumers seeking affordable products or rare items.
- **Best For**: Second-hand goods, rare or unique items, and affordable fashion. Mercari is well-suited for brands or

sellers looking to appeal to budget-conscious or trend-focused consumers.

ZOZOTOWN

ZOZOTOWN is Japan's leading fashion marketplace, catering to consumers who prioritise quality and style. Known for its extensive collection of fashion brands, ZOZOTOWN appeals to trend-conscious shoppers.

- **Advantages**: ZOZOTOWN's focus on fashion, combined with its high-quality presentation, attracts style-conscious buyers. The platform also offers a variety of Japanese and international brands.
- **Best For**: Clothing, accessories, shoes, and fashion-forward items. It's particularly suitable for fashion brands looking to establish a presence among Japanese fashion enthusiasts.

7.2 Crafting a Localised Marketing Strategy

To resonate with Japanese consumers, it's crucial to create a localised online presence that aligns with their expectations and cultural preferences. This includes adapting your website, optimising for Japanese search engines, and tailoring digital marketing efforts.

Website Localisation and SEO

Creating a Japanese-language website or localised section on your existing site can help engage Japanese consumers and improve search engine visibility.

- **Japanese Language**: Ensure that all site content, product descriptions, and customer service information are in Japanese. A professionally translated, culturally adapted website will create a positive impression and enhance user experience.
- **SEO on Yahoo! Japan and Google**: While Google is widely used, Yahoo! Japan is still popular in Japan, so

optimising for both search engines is essential. Focus on relevant Japanese keywords, create high-quality content, and consider link-building strategies with local sites to improve visibility.

- **Mobile Optimisation**: Since many Japanese consumers use smartphones for shopping, ensure your site is fully optimised for mobile. Prioritise fast loading times, clear navigation, and easy checkout options to improve mobile user experience.

Social Media Marketing

Social media is a powerful tool for connecting with Japanese consumers. Platforms like Instagram, Twitter, and LINE are popular for product discovery, brand engagement, and customer support.

- **Instagram**: Instagram is widely used for visual content and product discovery in Japan. High-quality images, interactive stories, and hashtags can help attract followers. Setting up an Instagram Shop can also facilitate direct sales.
- **Twitter**: Twitter is commonly used in Japan for real-time updates, promotions, and customer interaction. Using Twitter effectively involves frequent updates, responding to questions, and engaging with trending topics.
- **LINE**: LINE, Japan's most popular messaging app, offers business tools such as LINE Official Accounts, which allow brands to connect with followers, send updates, and offer promotions. LINE's reach and popularity make it a valuable platform for engaging directly with consumers.

Influencer Marketing

Influencer marketing is an effective strategy in Japan, especially in beauty, fashion, and tech sectors. Collaborating with influencers who align with your brand values can boost visibility and credibility.

- **Choosing the Right Influencers**: Select influencers whose audience and style align with your brand. In Japan, both macro-influencers (those with large followings) and micro-influencers (with smaller, highly engaged audiences) can be effective.
- **Campaigns and Promotions**: Popular influencer campaigns include product reviews, "unboxing" videos, and sponsored posts. Consider collaborating on giveaways or product launches to increase engagement and reach.

7.3 Payment Methods and Secure Transactions

Offering convenient, secure payment options is essential in Japan, where consumers expect flexibility and reliability in online transactions. Ensuring a range of local payment options can help you reach a broader audience and build trust.

Popular Payment Methods in Japan

- **Credit and Debit Cards**: Most Japanese consumers use credit or debit cards for online purchases, with Visa, Mastercard, and JCB being the most widely accepted.
- **Convenience Store Payments (Konbini)**: Convenience store payments, or "konbini" payments, are unique to Japan and allow customers to pay for online purchases at convenience stores like 7-Eleven and Lawson. This option is popular for those without credit cards or for added security.
- **Mobile Payments (e.g., PayPay, LINE Pay)**: Mobile payment solutions are growing in popularity, especially among younger consumers. Integrating mobile payment options like PayPay, Rakuten Pay, or LINE Pay can enhance customer convenience.

Secure Transactions and Trust Signals

Japanese consumers value security and trust when shopping online. Displaying trust signals and offering secure transaction methods can help boost your credibility.

- **SSL Certificates**: Ensure your website is secured with an SSL certificate to encrypt data and protect customer information.
- **Trust Badges**: Displaying trust badges from reputable sources, such as PayPal, Verisign, or McAfee, can reassure customers of your site's security.
- **Customer Reviews**: Japanese consumers rely heavily on reviews when making purchasing decisions. Incorporate customer testimonials and product ratings on your site to build trust and credibility.

7.4 Shipping and Logistics for Japanese Consumers

Japanese consumers expect fast, reliable, and flexible delivery options. Meeting these expectations can help you build a strong reputation in Japan's competitive e-commerce market.

Domestic Shipping Solutions

- **Japan Post**: Japan Post is the national postal service and offers reliable and affordable options for domestic deliveries. It's suitable for small-to-medium parcels and offers services like express delivery and international shipping.
- **Private Couriers**: Private courier companies like **Yamato Transport (Kuroneko)** and **Sagawa Express** offer high-quality services, including next-day and same-day delivery. They also provide refrigerated and temperature-controlled options for perishable goods.

Flexible Delivery Options

Japanese consumers value flexibility in delivery. Options like click-and-collect at convenience stores or lockers are increasingly popular, particularly among urban consumers.

- **Konbini Pick-Up**: Many online retailers partner with convenience stores, allowing customers to pick up their parcels at stores like 7-Eleven or FamilyMart, offering added convenience and flexibility.
- **Lockers and Drop-Off Points**: Delivery lockers are widely available in urban areas, allowing consumers to pick up their parcels at any time. This service is especially popular in Tokyo and other large cities.

Return Policies and Customer Support

- **Flexible Return Policies**: Japanese consumers expect clear and flexible return policies. Offering a 7–14 day return window, with simple return procedures, can enhance customer satisfaction.
- **Efficient Customer Support**: Ensure that customer service is responsive and available in Japanese. Prompt and courteous responses are highly valued and can lead to repeat purchases.

Chapter 7 - Summary

Selling online in Japan offers numerous opportunities, but success requires a thoughtful approach to localisation, customer service, and logistics. By choosing the right e-commerce platform, offering convenient payment options, and optimising for local search engines and mobile use, you can create a seamless shopping experience tailored to Japanese consumers' preferences. Secure, flexible delivery options and attentive customer service will further enhance your brand's reputation in Japan's competitive e-commerce market, helping you build a loyal customer base.

CHAPTER 8: MARKETING STRATEGIES FOR JAPANESE CONSUMERS

Marketing to Japanese consumers requires a strategic blend of digital engagement, localisation, and attention to detail. Japanese consumers are discerning, loyal, and expect brands to provide high-quality, consistent experiences across all channels. This chapter explores the key marketing strategies for reaching Japanese consumers, including the most effective digital channels, influencer collaborations, and traditional advertising methods.

8.1 Understanding Japanese Buyer Behaviour

Japanese consumers are known for their brand loyalty, high expectations of quality, and appreciation of excellent customer service. Understanding the unique characteristics of Japanese buyer behaviour will help you tailor your marketing strategy effectively.

Brand Loyalty and Trust

Japanese consumers are selective and tend to be loyal to brands that deliver consistent quality and reliability. Once they find a brand they trust, they are likely to remain loyal, particularly if the brand continues to meet or exceed their expectations.

- **Key Insight**: Building brand loyalty in Japan takes time and dedication. Consistency in quality, transparency, and strong customer service are essential for establishing a trustworthy brand that Japanese consumers will return to.

Attention to Detail and Quality

Quality is paramount to Japanese consumers, who expect products to be crafted with precision and care. This attention to detail also extends to the brand experience, from packaging to after-sales service.

- **Key Insight**: Emphasise quality and craftsmanship in your marketing materials, showcasing any unique or artisanal elements of your products. Ensuring your packaging reflects the high quality of your product can enhance customer satisfaction.

Preference for Personalisation

Japanese consumers appreciate personalised experiences and are more likely to respond positively to brands that tailor their offerings to individual preferences.

- **Key Insight**: Offering personalised recommendations, curated content, or customisable product options can help your brand stand out. Digital channels that allow for targeted marketing, such as email and social media, are excellent tools for delivering personalisation.

8.2 Digital Marketing Channels

Digital marketing is one of the most effective ways to reach Japanese consumers, who are highly engaged online. Below are the main channels to consider for creating a well-rounded digital marketing strategy in Japan.

SEO on Yahoo! Japan and Google

In Japan, both Yahoo! Japan and Google are widely used search engines, so optimising for both platforms is crucial for visibility.

- **Japanese Keywords**: Perform keyword research specific to Japanese language and culture. Optimise for Japanese phrases that align with consumer search behaviour, and include relevant local keywords to improve search engine rankings.
- **Content Localisation**: Use Japanese-language content

on your website and blog to increase visibility on Yahoo! Japan and Google. Blogging on topics related to your product, industry trends, or seasonal themes can also help attract more organic traffic.

Social Media Marketing

Social media is an essential part of daily life in Japan, and platforms such as Instagram, Twitter, and LINE are highly popular for product discovery, brand engagement, and customer interaction.

- **Instagram**: Instagram's visual nature is perfect for showcasing products, especially in the fashion, beauty, and lifestyle sectors. Use high-quality images, targeted hashtags, and Instagram Stories to boost engagement. Setting up an Instagram Shop can simplify the purchase process.

- **Twitter**: Twitter is widely used for real-time updates, promotions, and customer engagement. Japanese users are highly active on Twitter, making it an effective platform for product announcements, limited-time offers, and interacting directly with customers.

- **LINE**: As Japan's leading messaging app, LINE is a powerful tool for brands to connect with consumers. LINE Official Accounts allow businesses to send updates, promotions, and customer service messages directly to followers. This direct communication channel helps build a loyal customer base.

Content Marketing and Blogging

Content marketing is a valuable strategy for engaging Japanese consumers, who are highly receptive to informative and quality content. Blogs, articles, and product guides can help establish your brand as a trusted authority.

- **Naver Blog and Yahoo! Knowledge**: Naver Blog (popular in South Korea) and Yahoo! Knowledge are commonly used for product research in Japan, with consumers often seeking trusted sources. Consider creating content on these platforms to reach an informed audience.

- **Educational Content**: Blog posts or articles that explain the benefits of your product, how it's made, or provide usage tips can enhance trust. Japanese consumers appreciate detail, so providing in-depth information can create a positive brand impression.

8.3 Influencer Marketing in Japan

Influencer marketing is highly effective in Japan, where social media personalities and celebrities significantly impact consumer trends. Collaborating with influencers who align with your brand can boost visibility and enhance brand credibility.

Choosing the Right Influencers

Selecting influencers who resonate with your brand values and target audience is key. Both macro-influencers (with large followings) and micro-influencers (smaller, highly engaged audiences) are effective, depending on your budget and goals.

- **Macro-Influencers**: Collaborating with well-known personalities, especially in beauty, fashion, or tech sectors, can help increase brand visibility among a broad audience. These influencers are often popular on platforms like Instagram and YouTube.
- **Micro-Influencers**: Micro-influencers may have fewer followers, but their audiences are often highly engaged and loyal. They tend to focus on niche interests and can be effective for targeting specific demographics, such as eco-conscious consumers or tech enthusiasts.

Influencer Campaign Ideas

- **Product Reviews and Tutorials**: Partner with influencers to create product reviews, tutorials, or "how-to" videos. This content is popular among Japanese consumers, who prefer to research products thoroughly before purchasing.

- **Giveaways and Promotions**: Running giveaways or promotions with influencers can help increase brand awareness and drive engagement. Consider offering followers discounts or hosting a "like and follow" competition to grow your social media presence.
- **Collaborative Content**: Japanese consumers are responsive to authenticity, so collaborative content that feels genuine and informative often performs well. Influencers can create content that incorporates your product naturally, showing its real-life use and benefits.

8.4 Traditional Marketing Methods

While digital marketing is highly effective, traditional marketing methods, such as print advertising, TV commercials, and outdoor advertising, are still influential in Japan, particularly when targeting certain demographics.

Print Advertising

Print advertising is effective for reaching older consumers and professionals, especially through magazines and newspapers with a focus on lifestyle, fashion, and technology.

- **Best For**: Luxury products, high-quality goods, and niche markets. Print ads in high-circulation magazines or industry-specific publications can enhance your brand's prestige and visibility among a target audience.

Television Advertising

TV remains a popular medium in Japan, with a wide range of programmes and news channels attracting significant viewership. Television advertising can help build mass awareness and is particularly effective for large-scale brand campaigns.

- **Best For**: Mass-market products, seasonal promotions, and building brand recognition. Japanese consumers are known for their loyalty to familiar brands, so regular exposure through TV can solidify brand recognition.

Outdoor Advertising

Billboards, transit ads, and posters in high-traffic areas are common in Japan, especially in urban centres like Tokyo and Osaka. Outdoor advertising helps build brand awareness and promotes specific products or events.

- **Best For**: Urban locations, seasonal promotions, and events. Outdoor advertising is particularly effective near train stations, shopping districts, and tourist spots where foot traffic is high.

8.5 Combining Digital and Traditional Marketing

For maximum impact, consider a multi-channel approach that combines both digital and traditional marketing. Japanese consumers respond well to consistent messaging across multiple channels, and an integrated strategy can help reinforce brand awareness and build trust.

Examples of Multi-Channel Campaigns

- **Product Launches**: Launch new products with a combination of social media announcements, influencer partnerships, and targeted print or outdoor ads. This approach reaches diverse demographics and builds excitement around the launch.
- **Seasonal Campaigns**: During major Japanese holidays, such as New Year or Obon, combine social media promotions, LINE messaging, and in-store displays or print ads. Seasonal campaigns align with cultural events and can attract consumers looking for festive purchases.
- **Loyalty and Retention Programmes**: Use digital channels to engage customers with loyalty offers or exclusive discounts, while supplementing these efforts with in-store promotions or print ads. Loyalty programmes resonate with Japanese consumers, who value consistency and repeat purchases.

Chapter 8 - Summary

To successfully market to Japanese consumers, a well-rounded strategy that includes both digital and traditional channels is essential. Digital platforms like Instagram, LINE, and influencer marketing allow for direct engagement and personalised communication, while traditional channels like print and TV enhance brand visibility and reach a broader audience. By understanding Japanese buyer behaviour, including the importance of brand loyalty, quality, and personalisation, your brand can build meaningful connections and foster long-term success in Japan's competitive market.

CHAPTER 9: NAVIGATING JAPANESE BUSINESS ETIQUETTE

Japanese business culture places a high value on formality, respect, and professionalism. Understanding Japanese business etiquette is essential for establishing credibility and fostering strong relationships with Japanese partners, clients, and customers. This chapter provides insights into key aspects of Japanese business etiquette, from communication styles and meeting conduct to dress codes and the importance of building long-term relationships.

9.1 Formality and Respect in Business Interactions

In Japan, business interactions are often formal, and respect is a cornerstone of all professional relationships. Japanese business etiquette is rooted in hierarchy, which is typically determined by seniority, age, or job title.

Hierarchy and Titles

Japanese business culture respects hierarchy, and this respect is reflected in the use of titles rather than first names.

- **Using Titles**: Address colleagues and clients by their titles (e.g., Director Tanaka, Manager Suzuki) rather than by their first names. It's common to use titles even after multiple meetings, as this shows respect.
- **Respect for Seniority**: Deference to seniority is an important aspect of Japanese culture. Show particular respect for older individuals and higher-ranking colleagues. Allow senior members to initiate conversation or direct the flow of meetings.

Politeness and Communication Style

Japanese communication style is typically indirect, with an emphasis on politeness, modesty, and avoiding confrontation. Understanding this style can help prevent misunderstandings and make a positive impression.

- **Indirect Communication**: Japanese professionals may avoid saying "no" directly. Phrases like "it may be difficult" or "we'll consider it" are often polite ways to express hesitation or decline. Be mindful of these subtleties when interpreting responses.
- **Active Listening**: Use polite affirmations like "hai" (yes) or "so desu ne" (I see) to show engagement and understanding without interrupting. Japanese people appreciate good listeners, and nodding or providing quiet affirmations demonstrates attentiveness.
- **Avoiding Confrontation**: Avoid expressing disagreement or criticism openly, as it may cause embarrassment. If there is an issue, address it in private or use gentle language to avoid confrontation.

9.2 Business Meetings and Networking

Meetings and networking events in Japan follow structured, formal protocols. Punctuality, clear communication, and courteous behaviour are essential for leaving a positive impression in these settings.

Punctuality

Punctuality is highly valued in Japanese business culture and is considered a sign of respect and reliability.

- **Arriving Early**: Aim to arrive a few minutes early for meetings and appointments. Being on time is important, but arriving slightly early shows preparedness and respect.
- **Ending on Time**: Japanese professionals often follow strict schedules, so meetings generally conclude as planned. Be mindful of time and avoid overstaying

unless invited to continue.

Meeting Conduct

Japanese meetings are typically structured and agenda-driven, beginning with formal introductions and often including a degree of small talk to establish rapport.

- **Exchanging Business Cards**: Exchanging business cards, or "meishi," is an important part of Japanese business protocol. Offer and receive cards with both hands, and take a moment to examine the card before putting it away. Keep business cards visible on the table during the meeting as a sign of respect.
- **Formal Introductions**: Introductions are usually made in order of seniority, with the highest-ranking person introducing themselves first. Pay close attention to each introduction and respond with a polite bow.
- **Sticking to the Agenda**: Japanese meetings tend to be efficient and focused on the agenda. Stick to the planned topics and be prepared to answer detailed questions or provide supporting data as needed.

Networking Events

Networking is a valuable part of Japanese business culture, and social events are often used to strengthen business relationships.

- **Business Cards and Contact Information**: Bring plenty of business cards to networking events, as they are commonly exchanged. Be prepared to discuss your role and company in a clear, concise manner.
- **Follow-Up**: Follow up promptly with contacts after networking events, either with an email or a thank-you note. Express appreciation for their time and reiterate your interest in potential collaboration.

9.3 Dress Codes in Japanese Business Settings

Japanese business attire is generally conservative and formal, with an emphasis on professionalism and understated elegance. Dressing appropriately can help you make a positive impression.

Formal Business Attire

In most business settings, formal attire is the norm. Japanese professionals expect neat, well-fitted, and conservative clothing.

- **Men's Attire**: Men typically wear dark suits in neutral colours, such as black, navy, or grey, paired with a white or light-coloured dress shirt and a tie. Avoid flashy colours or patterns, as they are generally considered inappropriate.
- **Women's Attire**: Women often wear suits, dresses, or blouses with skirts or tailored trousers. Neutral or muted colours are preferred, and accessories should be minimal.

Business Casual

Business casual attire is sometimes acceptable, particularly in creative or tech industries, but it's still advisable to lean towards formal until you're sure of the dress code.

- **Men**: Business casual for men typically includes collared shirts, smart trousers, and a blazer. Ties are not always necessary in less formal settings.
- **Women**: Women may wear blouses, knee-length skirts, or tailored trousers, with minimal accessories. Avoid overly casual attire, even in more relaxed settings.

Regional and Industry Variations

In some industries, such as technology or media, dress codes may be slightly more relaxed. However, it's always best to err on the side of formality when meeting new clients or attending industry events.

9.4 Building Long-Term Business Relationships

Relationships are highly valued in Japan's business culture, and building trust with partners, clients, and colleagues is essential for long-term success. Japanese professionals prefer to work with people they know and trust, and establishing these connections can lead to mutually beneficial partnerships.

Commitment and Reliability

Reliability is a core value in Japanese business culture. Consistently meeting deadlines, following through on promises, and delivering high-quality work will help you earn the trust of Japanese colleagues and clients.

- **Delivering on Promises**: Avoid making promises you cannot keep, as Japanese professionals place a high value on dependability. Being reliable and consistent in your commitments will enhance your credibility.
- **Clear Communication**: Keep communication transparent and provide regular updates on projects, even if there are no new developments. Japanese partners appreciate being kept informed and will trust you more if they feel consistently updated.

Socialising Outside of Business

Socialising outside of formal business settings is an important way to build relationships in Japan. Dinners, after-work drinks, and other social gatherings are common and allow you to strengthen bonds with business partners on a more personal level.

- **Business Meals**: Meals are a common setting for informal business discussions. Wait for your host to initiate business talk, as they may prefer to start with casual conversation. Avoid discussing overly personal topics unless invited.
- **Drinking Culture**: Drinking is often a part of Japanese business culture, particularly in informal settings. If you drink, accept drinks poured by colleagues and reciprocate by pouring drinks for others. It's polite to participate, but you can decline if necessary; simply express gratitude and remain engaged in the

conversation.

- **Gift Giving**: Gift-giving is a respected custom in Japan, particularly around holidays like O-bon and New Year's. Small, thoughtful gifts are appreciated, especially if they are relevant to your home country or personal brand. Avoid overly expensive gifts, as they may make the recipient uncomfortable.

Respecting Privacy and Boundaries

While building relationships is essential, Japanese professionals also value privacy. Respect their boundaries and avoid prying into personal matters unless invited.

- **Personal Space**: Japanese people are generally respectful of personal space, so avoid physical contact beyond handshakes. Let them set the tone for any less formal greetings.
- **Professional Distance**: In the early stages of a relationship, maintain a respectful distance and be mindful not to overstep boundaries. As relationships deepen, Japanese professionals may open up more, but it's crucial to let them lead this progression.

Chapter 9 - Summary

Navigating Japanese business etiquette requires a deep respect for formality, hierarchy, and cultural norms. By understanding the importance of titles, dressing appropriately, and adhering to meeting protocols, you can establish credibility and build positive relationships in Japan's business world. Building trust and fostering long-term relationships with Japanese clients and partners is key to success, and social interactions outside of business settings play an essential role in strengthening these connections. Respect for privacy, reliability, and a commitment to quality will help you thrive in Japan's professional landscape and create lasting partnerships.

CHAPTER 10: CONCLUSION – UNLOCKING SUCCESS IN JAPAN

Japan is a land of rich traditions, sophisticated consumer expectations, and boundless innovation. While the Japanese market is known for its discerning standards and unique cultural nuances, businesses that understand and respect these elements can find significant success. By adapting to Japanese preferences for quality, detail, and excellent customer service, companies can build strong brands and create lasting relationships in one of the world's most influential markets.

In this chapter, we'll summarise the key insights and strategies covered throughout this guide and outline essential steps for building a sustainable, successful business in Japan.

10.1 Key Takeaways for Travelling and Selling in Japan

This guide has explored each essential aspect of establishing a business presence and selling in Japan. Below are the most important insights to remember as you navigate the Japanese market.

Understanding Japanese Culture and Consumer Preferences

- **Quality and Detail**: Japanese consumers expect high standards in product quality and service. Emphasising these values in all aspects of your business, from product design to customer service, is critical.
- **Adapting to Local Preferences**: Japanese consumers have unique tastes and preferences, especially in areas like packaging, aesthetics, and product functionality. Take time to research and understand these preferences, tailoring your offerings to align with Japanese

expectations.

Travelling and Logistics in Japan

- **Efficient Transport Network**: Japan's extensive and reliable transport network makes it easy to travel and manage logistics. From the Shinkansen to local public transport, leveraging Japan's transport infrastructure will facilitate business activities and reduce operational challenges.

- **Reliable Shipping Options**: Japan offers various domestic shipping solutions, including Japan Post and private couriers like Yamato Transport. Fast, flexible shipping options are crucial in meeting Japanese consumers' high expectations for convenience and reliability.

Setting Up a Business in Japan

- **Choosing the Right Business Structure**: Select the business structure that best fits your goals, whether it's a sole proprietorship, limited liability company (Godo Kaisha), or corporation (Kabushiki Kaisha). Understanding the tax and administrative requirements of each structure is essential for long-term success.

- **Adhering to Consumer Protection Laws**: Japan has strict consumer protection regulations, including product safety, labelling, and data protection laws. Compliance with these regulations is vital for building trust and credibility with Japanese consumers.

Selling Online and in Markets

- **E-Commerce Opportunities**: Japan's thriving e-commerce market provides opportunities for growth, especially for brands that establish a localised digital presence. Platforms like Rakuten, Amazon Japan, and Yahoo! Shopping enable businesses to reach a large audience while catering to Japanese preferences for convenience and fast delivery.

- **Market and Fair Culture**: Japan's vibrant market scene offers a chance to connect directly with consumers, build brand awareness, and test new products. Whether you're selling in Tsukiji Market, Kyoto's Nishiki Market, or other local markets, a well-designed stall and culturally respectful approach are essential for success.

Effective Marketing Strategies

- **Digital Marketing and Social Media**: Leveraging digital channels like Instagram, Twitter, and LINE allows you to connect with Japanese consumers directly. Tailoring your social media presence and content to Japanese preferences helps build brand visibility and customer loyalty.

- **Influencer Marketing**: Collaborating with influencers who resonate with your brand values can significantly enhance credibility and reach. Influencers on platforms like Instagram and YouTube can help drive brand awareness, particularly in the fashion, beauty, and technology sectors.

Navigating Japanese Business Etiquette

- **Respect for Formality and Hierarchy**: Japanese business culture emphasises respect for hierarchy, formality, and professionalism. Adhering to these customs and demonstrating attentiveness to detail can establish credibility and foster strong business relationships.

- **Building Long-Term Relationships**: Patience and commitment are essential for establishing long-term relationships in Japan. Socialising outside formal business settings and consistently delivering quality work will help earn the trust of Japanese partners and clients.

10.2 Steps to Achieving Success in Japan

Following these key steps will help you establish and grow a successful business in Japan's competitive market.

1. Conduct Thorough Market Research

Understanding Japan's unique market characteristics is essential. Research Japanese consumer behaviour, local trends, and potential competitors to develop a strategy that aligns with Japan's demand for quality and innovation.

- **Stay Informed**: Keep up with changes in Japanese consumer trends, particularly in industries like fashion, beauty, tech, and food. Japan's market evolves rapidly, so staying informed will help you adapt and remain relevant.

2. Localise Your Brand and Products

Japanese consumers appreciate brands that understand their culture and preferences. Tailoring your brand image, product design, and messaging to the Japanese market will set you apart from competitors.

- **Localisation**: Provide Japanese-language content, adapt packaging and labelling to local standards, and consider Japanese preferences for aesthetics and functionality. Localising your products and brand message will enhance customer engagement and trust.

3. Build Strong Relationships and Maintain Consistency

Trust is fundamental in Japanese business culture. Consistently delivering on your promises and maintaining a reliable reputation will strengthen your relationships with Japanese clients, partners, and customers.

- **Reliability**: Japanese consumers and business partners value reliability. Focus on delivering consistent quality and service, and build a reputation for dependability in all aspects of your operations.

4. Implement a Multi-Channel Marketing Strategy

A diverse marketing approach, including social media, influencer partnerships, and traditional advertising, can help you reach a broader audience and establish brand recognition in Japan.

- **Integrate Digital and Traditional Marketing**: Use social media to engage with customers directly while supporting your efforts with print ads, TV commercials, or outdoor advertising, especially for brand awareness and seasonal campaigns.

5. Prioritise Customer Satisfaction

Japanese consumers are loyal but selective, often conducting extensive research before committing to a brand. Providing high-quality products, attentive customer service, and a positive experience will encourage repeat purchases and build customer loyalty.

- **After-Sales Support**: Follow up with customers after purchases, offer easy returns and exchanges, and ensure that customer service is available and responsive. Going the extra mile to support your customers can build loyalty and encourage referrals.

Final Thoughts: Unlocking Your Potential in Japan

Japan's sophisticated and discerning market offers tremendous opportunities for businesses willing to adapt and engage with Japanese culture. Achieving success in Japan is more than just introducing quality products—it's about understanding consumer expectations, respecting cultural nuances, and building strong, long-term relationships with customers and partners alike.

As you continue your journey in Japan, remember that consistency, quality, and attentiveness to detail will set you apart. With the insights and strategies provided in this guide, you are well-equipped to navigate Japan's unique business landscape and unlock the full potential of this influential market. Embrace the journey with patience and respect, and your brand will flourish in

Japan's competitive, rewarding environment.

Good luck with your venture in Japan, and may your business succeed and thrive as you unlock new opportunities in this extraordinary market!

ABOUT THE AUTHOR

J K Lewis

J K Lewis has spent the past 30 years working, travelling and successfully selling in countries all around the world. He has lived in the UK, Germany and in South Korea; business has taken him all around Europe, the US and America, Asia and the MEA region. His sales and marketing experience covers a wide range of Products  and Services, from High-value German Engineering, to UK made special machinery, American Quality Management Services, to Chinese packaging and labels.

www.ingramcontent.com/pod-product-compliance
Lightning Source LLC
Chambersburg PA
CBHW052339220526
45472CB00001B/493